KT-593-672

Michael Phelps

Roy Apps

Illustrated by Chris King

LONDON · SYDNEY

Chapter One:

Fight!

"Big Ears! Big Ears!"

The chanting started with just one kid, a pink, freckly boy wearing a back-to-front baseball cap. Then the rest of the children on the school bus started too. All the children, that is, except the one they called Big Ears.

"Big Ears! Big Ears!"

The boy they called Big Ears squirmed in his seat, desperately trying to turn away from the taunting.

Then he looked up and caught the glint of evil triumph in the face of the pink, freckly boy, who was behind him.

Suddenly, something inside him snapped. He turned around and thumped the freckly boy. Then he thumped him again and again, his anger and hurt feeding every punch he landed.

Around him the chants of "Big Ears!" quickly turned to cries of:

"Fight! Fight!"

The driver screeched to a halt. Everyone sat down. The driver walked through the bus until he reached the boy they called Big Ears.

"Michael Phelps," he drawled, putting his face right up close to him, "you are trouble. As soon as I get back to the depot, I'm gonna call the school and report you to the principal."

Chapter Two:

The Best Place in the World

Michael and his mother sat in front of the big desk in the principal's office.

"Fighting, especially on the school bus, is an issue which this school takes very seriously," said the principal. "You will be excluded from school for two days."

Michael fidgeted on his seat and began kicking the leg of the principal's desk with his foot. He couldn't stand being in there any longer. He just wanted to get out.

"Listen to me when I'm speaking to you, Michael," the principal snapped.

Michael carried on looking at the floor. He could feel the principal staring at him; his mum, too. He knew how worried she was about him.

"And how is being out of school for two days going to help Michael?" she asked the principal.

"Bad behaviour must be punished," replied the principal. "Besides, a two-day exclusion is neither here nor there when it comes to Michael's prospects."

Michael glanced up. His mum and the principal were squaring up for a fight, he could tell. His mum was good at dealing with teachers; after all, she was one herself.

"And what do you mean by that?" asked his mum sharply.

The principal shrugged. "Just that Michael is always fooling around in class."

"Maybe he's bored with lessons," replied his mum.

The principal smirked. "I can't see Michael ever being able to focus on anything in his life." He stood up. "Now, if you'll excuse me, I have important things to do."

Each day Michael was at home excluded from school, his mum made him sit down and do some school work. He did some English and some maths – he liked the maths better. When he'd done his schoolwork, he dashed out of the house straight away and ran down the road towards his local swimming pool.

The pool was the one place Michael felt really happy. A long rectangle with lanes at the sides, and black stripes on the bottom to help with your direction. He knew where he was going when he swam. That helped slow down his mind.

Michael hadn't always liked the pool. When he first went there, aged seven, he hated it. Really hated it.

"I'm cold! I'm not going in there! I don't want to get my face wet!" he screamed.

Eventually, the swimming teacher persuaded Michael to go in the water on his back so that he didn't get his face wet. That way he couldn't see just how deep the pool was, either.

Slowly, he got to quite like the water. When he began swimming at the deep end, where his feet couldn't reach the bottom, he knew that the pool was the best place in the world.

So when there was trouble at school, or all the stuff at home to do with his parents' divorce started to make him sad and anxious, he escaped to the pool.

The one place he felt safe; the one place he felt free.

Michael's older sisters, Whitney and Hilary, were keen swimmers, too. He used to have to go with them and his mum to swimming meets. One day, fed up with hanging around with a lot of girls, he found himself doing a bit of exploring.

Up by the parking lot, there was a huge trailer done out like a shop. It was full of everything to do with swimming: trunks, caps, goggles, towels and posters of the world's most famous swimmers. Michael stared at these posters. Two thoughts came into his mind: firstly, that the posters would look really cool on his bedroom wall. Secondly, that one day he'd like to be a famous swimmer and be featured on a wall poster.

Michael's mum bought him a poster. At every swimming meet he would look out for the trailer shop. Soon, he began spending most of his time there. He got to know the shop owner, whose name was Greg.

Michael would help Greg out, fetching stuff for customers and sorting out the right size caps or trunks. He would race around, dashing from one side of the shop to the other, running up and down the small set of steps, so that he could reach things on the top shelves. Nobody told him off for not sitting still.

Greg was happy to have Michael to help in his shop. "This is my business associate, Mr Phelps," he would tell his customers. It was kind of a joke, Michael knew, but when the customers laughed, it was a good sort of laugh.

One day, Michael said to Greg, "I'd like to be a world-famous swimmer."

Greg frowned. "That's some ambition," he said.

"Uh-oh, here we go," thought Michael. "Here's somebody else who's going to tell me I can't do anything because I have trouble concentrating."

Greg looked hard at Michael. "To be a top swimmer you've got to have commitment. Have you got commitment?"

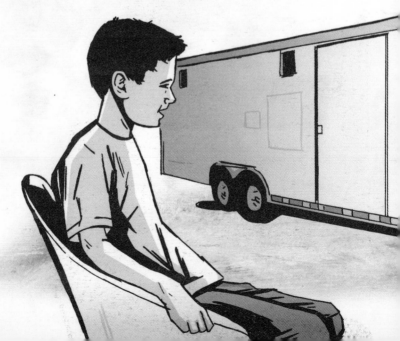

Michael frowned. "I think so," he said.

"Then there's no reason why you shouldn't become a top swimmer," Greg said, "especially if your swimming is anything as good as your sisters'." He grinned.

"Really?" asked Michael, quietly.

"Sure," said Greg. His face was serious. "I reckon you could make it all the way to the top. But whether you make it or not is down to you."

Chapter Three:

The Coach

Michael worked hard at his swimming. He started to win races. The trouble was, if he didn't win, he'd get really angry. Angry with the world, angry with himself. He'd shout, stomp about and throw his swimming goggles at the other kids. And he also had trouble concentrating. He had a condition called Attention Deficit Hyperactivity Disorder, or ADHD for short, and was taking medication called Ritalin to help him.

One day, a group of boys started throwing soap and towels around the changing rooms. One of the club coaches stormed in. His name was Bob Bowman. He didn't work with Michael's group; but he knew the name of the biggest troublemaker around.

"Michael Phelps!" he yelled. "Stop that!"

"It wasn't me!" Michael protested. But it was no good. Michael was the one with the bad reputation. Michael was the one who got told off. He stormed out, sulking. "I'm glad that idiot isn't my coach," he thought.

A few weeks later, Michael joined a new group for advanced swimmers. He was just eleven; two or three years younger than the others. He was really excited, until he found out that the coach for the advanced swimmers was Bob Bowman!

Bob Bowman wasn't too pleased to find Michael in the advanced group, either. His first thought was: "That kid won't last long. He's trouble. He can't focus on anything."

After the first training session, though, Bob Bowman was forced to admit to himself: "That kid is good. Very good!"

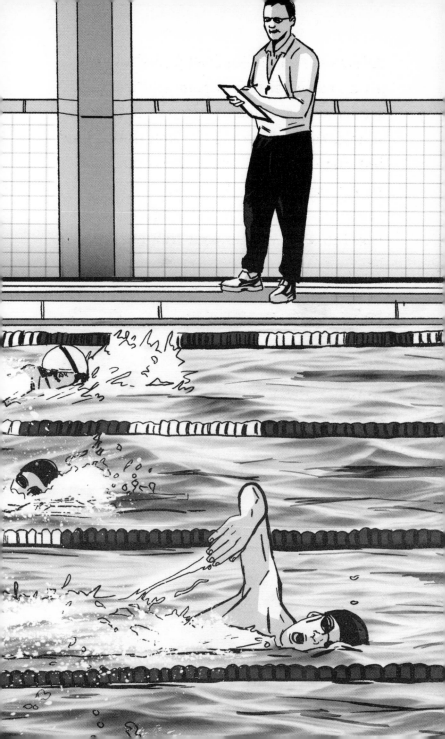

But Michael still didn't like being told what to do. One day, during training, he deliberately swam really slowly, so that the people behind him had to swim slowly, too. Bob called Michael out of the pool.

"That's it, Michael!" he fumed. "You're out of this club until you do your training properly."

Michael thought Bob was bluffing. He was the best swimmer in his group. They needed him if they were going to win competitions.

But he was wrong. Bob called Michael's parents and arranged to meet them with Michael at the pool at 5.30am the next day.

"Michael, you've got the talent to reach the top, but to get there you've got to have commitment," he said.

Michael remembered that Greg, the shop owner, had told him the same thing. He stood up and went down the stairs to the pool. It was only a quarter to six in the morning, but he did his training straight away – and properly this time, too.

Other times though, he was still likely to be found mucking about: chucking goggles, throwing towels, tipping swimming capfuls of water over people when they were changing – Michael did it all. He had ambition, but he didn't really have a dream.

In the summer of 1996 though, that all changed.

Chapter Four:

The Dream

In the summer of '96, Michael went with his family to the Olympic Games in Atlanta, Georgia. There he saw the American swimmers Tom Malchow and Tom Dolan win medals. There he began to dream of becoming an Olympic swimming champion himself.

But could he really win an Olympic medal? He was a good swimmer he knew, but he had ADHD and had real trouble concentrating on anything.

One day coming home from school he made a decision; a decision that he knew would worry his mum.

"Mum, I want to come off Ritalin," he said when he got in.

"But Michael, you know how hard you find it to concentrate."

"Mum, I'll concentrate harder."

His mum frowned. "Look Michael, if you do this and I start to get phone calls from school to say you've been misbehaving in class again…"

"Mum!" Michael's face was serious. "I've got to do this. It's time."

With his doctor's help, Michael was gradually weaned off Ritalin. It took a year until he was able to stop taking Ritalin completely.

But by then Michael knew what it was like to set yourself a difficult goal – and to achieve it.

Now he could focus on his big dream – to win an Olympic gold medal.

The next few years weren't easy. There were times when Michael let himself – and his coach – down. But he stuck at it. People at school stopped calling him Big Ears. Now his nickname was Squid Boy, but he didn't mind that one bit.

By 1999, when Michael was 14, he was good enough to take part in the trials for the 2000 Sydney Olympic Games. Only two swimmers would go through in each event, and for Michael taking part was really a chance to experience the atmosphere ready for when he was older.

On the second day he swam his first race and finished 11th. He had one other event left, the 200m fly. He did better in this race and after 150m was in 5th place; a long way off the leaders, but a good effort nevertheless.

Michael's mum left her seat and went downstairs to the pool, so she could be there at the end of the race to tell her son how proud she was of him. So she didn't see the last 50m of the race: 50m in which Michael put on an incredible burst of speed.

The first hand to touch the finishing wall belonged to the swimmer Michael had admired three years before in Atlanta, Georgia: the defending Olympic silver medalist, Tom Malchow. The second hand to touch the finishing wall, one sixth of a second after Tom Malchow's, was Michael's.

It was the only time in his swimming career that he was proud to come second, because it meant that he was in the US Olympic swimming team; the youngest male swimmer in the team for 68 years.

Was his dream of becoming an Olympic medalist about to come true?

Chapter Five:

Olympic Games

For Michael, the preparations for the Olympic Games were a whirl. As well as training, there were medicals and media interviews. A 15-year-old representing the United States at the Olympic Games! It was a great story.

As the plane circled over Sydney Harbour, Australia, Michael and two other young members of the US Olympic team were invited up into the cockpit. They got a pilot's-eye-view of the famous skyline.

When it came to the big race, Michael swam well, beating his personal best by half a second, but it wasn't good enough. He finished 5th, a full 0.33 of a second behind the bronze medalist.

After the race, his fellow American in the team, Tom Malchow, who had won gold, came up to him and patted him on the back.

"Michael, your best is yet to come," the older swimmer told him.

In his disappointment, Michael found this difficult to believe. All the frenzied preparations, the training, the excitement had led to… nothing. No journalists were interested in interviewing him now. He flew back home early.

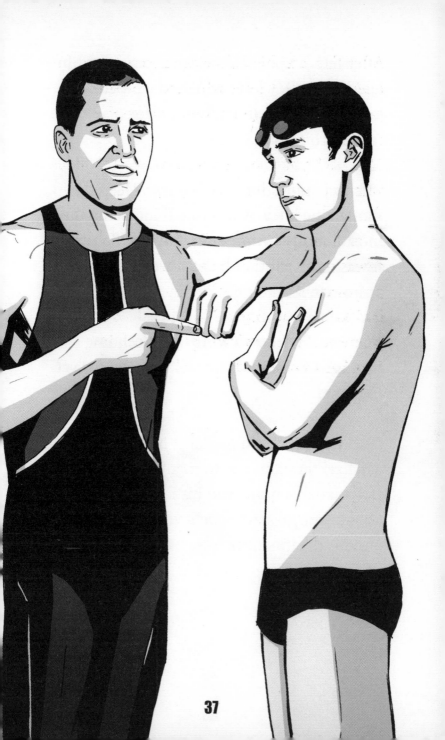

Michael's school held a special party for him and his English teacher played a practical joke, pretending to tell him off for playing truant from so many lessons.

Michael enjoyed it all, of course. Deep down, though, he knew it was one thing being the most famous swimmer in Towson, Baltimore; it was quite another being a world-famous swimmer.

But Tom Malchow's words kept echoing through his mind: "Michael, your best is yet to come."

If an Olympic gold medalist believed in him, Michael thought, not to mention Bob Bowman, his mum and his family, it was about time he started believing in himself and his dream again, too.

Chapter Six:

Record Breaker!

In the autumn of 2000, Michael had a big row with Bob Bowman. They had both been disappointed by the Olympics and were both feeling really down after all the excitement and hard work that had gone into training. They argued about commitment, about attitude, about everything. Furniture was kicked and books were thrown.

Once the air had cleared, one thing became obvious to both of them: the next Olympics were four years off. Michael needed a goal to reach before that. They decided on the National Swimming Championships which were being held in six months' time. Michael's goal was to become a national champion.

For the next six months Michael trained hard. He was fitter and faster than ever. He would need to beat Tom Malchow to become national champion, though.

Throughout the race, Michael was behind Tom. Then with just 25 metres left, he made one of his famous surges. His hand touched the finishing wall first. He stayed in the pool, just floating there for a second, before becoming aware of the huge excited roar from the crowd above him.

Then he looked up and saw the board had recorded his time as 1:54:92. He had not only become national champion, he had broken the world record. The youngest person ever to do so.

Michael climbed out of the pool and waved at the cheering crowds. His dream of Olympic gold was well and truly on.

Fact file
Michael Phelps

* Full name: Michael Fred Phelps II

* Born: Baltimore, Maryland, USA, 30 June 1985

* Height: 1.93 metres

* Weight: 91 kilograms

1992–95	Starts swimming, aged 7 and by the age of 10 already holds a national record for his age group.
1996	Aged 11, starts to train at the North Baltimore Aquatic Club under coach Bob Bowman.
2000	Aged 15 competes at the 2000 Olympics in Sydney, the youngest American male swimmer at an Olympic Games in 68 years.
2001	Sets world record in the 200m butterfly; the youngest male swimmer in history to ever set a swimming world record.
2002	Establishes new world record for the 400m individual medley.
2004	Breaks his own world record in the 400m individual medley during the US trials for the 2004 Summer Olympics. Olympic Games, Athens: six gold medals (including two world records) and two bronze medals. Street in his hometown of Baltimore is renamed Michael Phelps Way.
2005	World Championships, Canada: five gold medals.
2007	World Championships, Melbourne, Australia: seven gold medals, including five world records.
2008	Olympic Games, Beijing, China: eight gold medals, the most won by any competitor ever in the Olympic Games. It also means he has a total of 14 gold medals, the most ever won by an Olympian.
2009	Appears before the Maryland House of Delegates and the Maryland Senate to be honoured for his Olympic accomplishments.

Rebecca Adlington

The 14-year-old girl stood on the side of the pool in the final of the 2003 European Youth Olympics 800 metres freestyle. As the swimmers dived in, the arena echoed noisily with shouts and cheers from the spectators. "Come on, Becks!" shouted the girl's family from their seats in the crowd. The girl touched the finishing wall in second place. Afterwards, her family and friends crowded around to congratulate her for winning the silver medal. A man approached the girl's mum. "That was a brilliant race your daughter swam," he said. "I think she's got potential. My name's Bill Furniss, by the way. I'm a professional swimming coach and I'd like to offer to coach your daughter."

**Continue reading this story in
DREAM TO WIN: Rebecca Adlington**

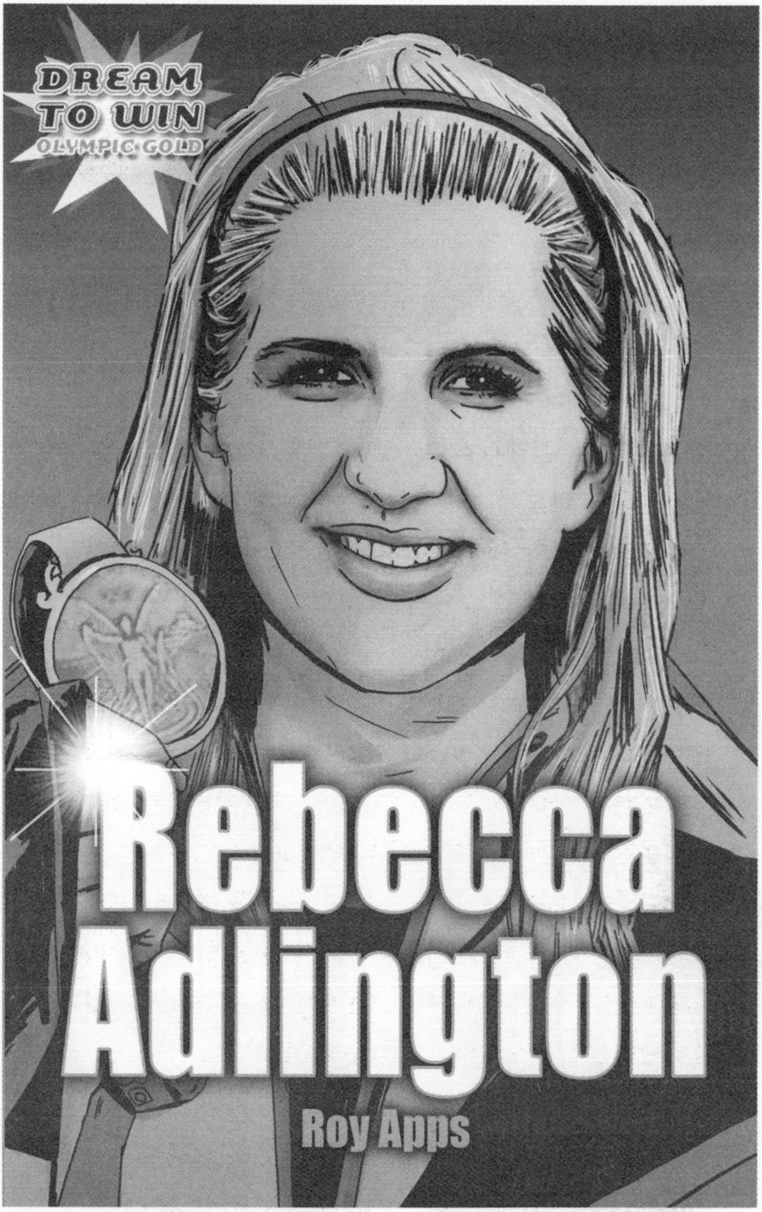
DREAM
TO WIN
OLYMPIC GOLD
Rebecca
Adlington
Roy Apps

Also by Roy Apps,
published by Franklin Watts:

978 0 7496 7057 3

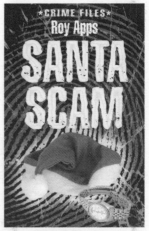

978 0 7496 7056 6

978 0 7496 7054 2

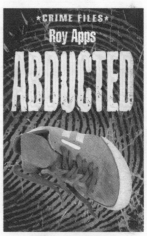

978 0 7496 7053 5